MW01094582

365
WAYS
To Get Along
WITH YOUR
COLLEGE
ROOMMATE

52 WAYS To Get Along WITH YOUR COLLEGE ROOMMATE

C. E. Rollins

OLIVER NELSON

THOMAS NELSON PUBLISHERS
Nashville · Atlanta · London · Vancouver

Published in Nashville, Tennessee, by Thomas Nelson, Inc., Publishers, and distributed in Canada by Word Communications, Ltd., Richmond, British Columbia.

Library of Congress Cataloging-in-Publication Data

Rollins, Catherine E., 1950–
    52 ways to get along with your college roommate / C.E. Rollins.
        p.   cm.
    ISBN 0-8407-9261-1 (pbk.)
    1. Roommates—Life skills guides.   2. College students—Life skills guides.   3. Interpersonal relations.   I. Title.   II. Title: Fifty-two ways to get along with your college roommate.
HQ975.R65   1994
646.7—dc20   94-4726
                                                                      CIP

Printed in the United States of America.

1   2   3   4   5   6   —   99   98   97   96   95   94

To
my former roommates
Barbara, Geri, Kathy, Ursula,
Twila, and Beverly

❏ Contents

Good Roommate Do's and Don'ts

Parting Company

❑ Introduction

The vast majority of roommates are temporary.

That's the good news for many people, who find themselves with less-than-ideal roommates or with roommate relationships that have soured.

For others, that's the bad news—the sad fact that a good roommate relationship must come to an end as life paths take different twists and turns.

For *all* roommates, the temporary nature of most roommate relationships is a fact of life that should be faced at the outset of a rooming-together circumstance. In facing up to and talking openly about the temporary nature of the situation that brings two people to share living quarters and, thus, their lives, both parties tend to order their own space, identify their own needs, and occupy their part of the relationship a little more realistically and objectively. It's also a fact that's helpful to remember when difficulties arise: "This, too, can be endured since it's only for a while."

Given that caveat, sharing space with a roommate—for however brief or long a time—provides an opportunity for *relationship*. And being in relationship offers each person an opportunity to learn more about how to understand self, how to communicate, how to give and receive, and how to build trust. Some roommate relationships become deep friendships that outlast a living-together situation for many years. Other roommate relationships start out superficial and remain so.

It is perhaps important, therefore, at the beginning of a book such as this to recognize some important differences between roommate relationships and friendships:

- Friendships tend to be built on common interests, shared experiences, and like values and beliefs. Roommates occupy the same dwelling place and are very often placed together (by lottery, alphabetical order, or dorm director whim), and they may know very little, if anything, about each other.

- A friendship may arise from a roommate situation, but friendship is not an automatic by-product of living together. Even enemies can learn to coinhabit a space peacefully. Conversely, friends aren't always the best people to choose as roommates if given the option to do so. Sometimes friends remain closer if a little distance is built into their relationship. In sum, don't assume that your roommate automatically will be your friend or that a friend will be a good roommate.

- Friendship is based on a mutual liking. Roommate relationships are based on mutual space. Thus, friendships are internal in their motivation and growth. Roommate relationships are rooted in the external facts of life and, as such, are much more prone to rule making and boundary setting.

Think temporary. Think external and objective. And the 52 ideas here will make a great deal more sense and be much easier to apply.

The hope, nonetheless, is that you will be fortunate to find roommates who become friends with whom you can share more than a refrigerator or a closet—friends with whom you can share your laughter and tears, your joys and sorrows, and the deepest secrets of your heart.

1 ❑ Up-Front Agreements

Review the Basics From the first hour with a new roommate—whether it is the first time you meet each other or the first time you walk into a new space that you intend to share—talk about the fact that you need to have an agreement that will cover these basics.

Who is going to provide what This discussion should cover initial furnishings, supplies, and ongoing consumables.

Who is going to pay for what Include who is going to provide the money for which bills (including down payments) and how you are going to share mutual expenses and in what proportion.

Who is going to do what Cover the basics of chores and responsibilities for the cleaning and ongoing maintenance of your shared space.

How long the first round of your living together is going to last Anticipate in advance when your roommate relationship might end. Semester end? Term end? Don't assume that you'll be roommates throughout college or even for a full school year. Anticipate that both may want a change, and talk about when that first shift may occur. Saying, "Let's see how it goes," leaves both roommates only half-settled mentally and emotionally.

Agree to Agree   Agree about the importance of agreeing. Set a time—if that first hour isn't convenient—when you can get together and come up with a very basic agreement that, in essence, will be the covenant between you regarding the space you are occupying.

Don't assume that because you are friends or good acquaintances that you will be able to work out any difference of opinion later or that there's no need for this. No matter how good your friendship may be, an agreement about your living arrangement will only make it better. If the friendship can't stand up to the very simple rigors of agreeing on basic protocol and possessions, perhaps you shouldn't be roommates!

That leads us to a key principle: if you can't agree to agree, there's little on which to build a successful roommate relationship. Bail out early. You'll save yourself a great deal of frustration, time, and perhaps money.

Find Out About Landlord Agreements
Whether you are occupying a dorm room, a room in a fraternity or sorority house, or an apartment, make certain that you and your roommate have an initial check of the space in which you are going to live with the person in charge of assigning you or leasing you that space. Check for defects in the

structure of the room or apartment—for example, holes in walls, windows that can't be opened, cracked light fixtures, missing vent covers, major spots on walls or carpeting. You don't want to be charged for these damages later and find yourself without proof that you weren't responsible. Get this up-front appraisal *in writing.*

Also check that any appliances or heating and cooling units are in good working order. Turn on the furnace (even if it's sweltering outside). Turn on the air conditioner (even if it's freezing). Do all the burners on the stove heat? Does the toilet flush? Do the sinks drain?

Go over any rules, regulations, payment dates, and other stipulations of your room agreement or lease with the person in charge. This has a dual purpose: you become thoroughly familiar with what is going to be required of you, and you know that your roommate is familiar with the rules and regulations regarding your living together.

Reappraise the Initial Agreement Establish a time when you agree to reappraise your initial agreement. You might say, "Let's talk this over again six weeks from today once we see how things are working." (Put the date and time on your calendars.) Part of your agreeing to agree should include the decision to agree on midcourse corrections.

Agreeing to agree is starting out on the right foot in a roommate relationship. And now for some specifics about which to reach agreement.

2 ❏ Deciding What to Share

In forging an agreement, some of the basics that you should face immediately are decisions about what you will share and what will be off-limits to each other. Don't *assume* that you know what is mutual property or that your roommate knows what shouldn't be touched. Talk it out.

Shared Expenses Are you sharing expenses? Which ones? Equally?

Don't limit your discussion to rent. Who will pay for the utilities and in what proportion? (If one person travels a great deal and the other has more use of the shared space, are you going to resent that person paying only half of the utilities? Should utilities be prorated in such a case on a daily access basis?)

Who will pay for cable television or home delivery of a daily newspaper?

Who will pay for space-related upkeep and consumable items? There's no need for both roommates to supply a can of furniture polish or bottle of window cleaner. Who will pay what?

If repairs are needed, who will pay?

If one person can't pay this month, who will pay?

If you are a neatnik and your roommate a slob, and your roommate wants to hire a maid, who will pay?

If you are willing to mow the lawn and take care of the flower beds, should your roommate pay for the mower gasoline and buy the bedding plants?

Shared Legal Responsibility Are both of you signing the lease, mortgage, or room agreement? What happens if one person moves out prior to the end of the term? Is the other person fully responsible for expenses, or does the moving-out roommate have some liability?

Shared Chores Are you responsible only for keeping up your room, or do you have responsibility for cleaning other rooms of a larger house in which you are living? What are your chores? How often are you responsible for doing those chores? Who makes sure the room is ready for clean room check?

Shared Possessions Is each person contributing possessions to the new environment? Are they going to be shared or kept mutually exclusive?

Shared Decision Making Who gets to make decorating decisions? Who decides if you'll share your space with a pet or houseplants? Who makes out the weekly chore schedule? Who decides if something is dirty or clean, if the channel on the radio should be changed, or if the utility bills are too high and the thermostat needs to be permanently lowered (or raised)?

Anticipate as many situations as you can, and reach agreements that seem fair to both of you.

3 ❏ Dividing the Space

Unless you walk into a roommate situation in which the other person has already moved into half of the room or apartment, consider the dividing of space to be the cornerstone of your agreement with a roommate.

Agree to agree about who gets which bedroom and bath, bed, dresser, or bookshelf unit. Who gets which half of the closet or which set of drawers?

You may want to toss a coin to give each person equal access to the better view or the more convenient location.

Take turns calling dibs on certain facets of the room. For example, if one person gets to choose which bed he wants, the other person should have the option of choosing which desk.

Kitchen Cupboards and Fridge   Extend the division of space into the kitchen area (if you have one). Consider having yours, mine, and ours shelves in the refrigerator and food cupboards.

Going Halves   In an ideal roommate situation, each person will have her own bedroom, bath, and parking space. If sharing a bedroom and bath, each person will have her own bed, desk, closet space, dresser, and bookshelf. If sharing a dresser or bookshelf, each person will have her own drawers or shelves—*in half!* Just because your roommate shows up with ten times more stuff than you have does not mean that she gets 90 percent of the space!

Storage Some things may need to go into storage. If you don't have sufficient room to store all of your things in half the space provided the two of you, recognize that you need to divest part of your current stash of worldly goods, get a storage locker, or send some items elsewhere.

Access to Space Agree to agree that certain mutual living areas need to be shared. One person shouldn't habitually spread out all his homework and snacks on the living room floor, hog the TV area, or take over the dining room table. Mutual space needs to remain mutual, used equally, and be subject to asking permission of the other person.

4 ❑ Dividing the Fixtures

The fixtures of living include appliances, items of furniture, and consumables that you will share.

Even dorm-room roommates frequently share one popcorn maker, one tiny refrigerator, one stereo unit, one television set, and one beanbag chair. Nearly all roommates who share a kitchen share one bottle of ketchup, one jar of mustard, and one tub of butter. Roommates who have responsibility for utilities may share electricity, water, natural gas, and garbage pickup fees. Discuss what is to be shared and what is to remain private.

Courtesy Use Rules Talk over with your roommate the wisdom of following some of these basic courtesy rules:

- If you use it, replace it (with like kind or quality).

- If you get it dirty, clean it thoroughly to the owner's satisfaction.

- If you break it, repair it professionally.

- If you borrow it, return it in good working order and to the exact place where you found it.

- If you have doubts about whether you should borrow it, ask first!

Off-Limits Items   Communicate openly with your roommate about what you do *not* want your roommate to use or borrow without your specific permission. Do you consider it a violation of your privacy for your roommate to go into your room or bathroom? Do you wish for your roommate to refrain completely from using your personal items (such as hair curlers or razor) or wearing your clothes? Do you want a roommate to keep his hands off your stereo or your collection of compact discs? Let your wishes be known up-front. (You need not feel selfish in the process. Your reasons for wanting certain possessions to be exclusively yours are your reasons.)

Expressing Value   Let your roommate know if certain items are valuable to you for sentimental reasons or if you want certain items to receive special care. If you don't want your roommate to put her shoes on your furniture or use your heirloom vase for flowers, say so.

5 ❏ Deciding Who Pays

In addition to various items requiring payment that have been discussed previously—such as rent, repairs, and shared consumables—several key decisions need to be made about the financial responsibilities of both parties.

Record Down Payments Keep a written record of who makes which down payments. You may think you'll remember, but when the phone company sends a refund twelve months after you move in, will you be able to prove who paid the initial deposit? The same goes for security and cleaning deposits.

Make Payments Decide who will be responsible for making sure that both rent checks get to the landlord's office on the day the rent is due or that both checks for the telephone are mailed on time to the phone company. Generally, one person in a roommate relationship needs to take the lead responsibility for making sure that monthly bills are paid on time and in full.

Divide the Bills Utility and food bills should be discussed periodically. Ideally, utility and food usage should be equal between roommates. Practically, that is rarely the case. In any given time frame, one roommate is likely to have eaten more out of the fridge or taken more showers and done more laundry. Talk initially and then periodically, if you need to, about the importance of being generous givers and reluctant users. If you know in your heart that you have consumed the lion's share of the utilities or pantry, offer to pay more than your usual half that month (or week). If you feel that you are being used to pay for the extravagance of a roommate, speak your mind, and reach a new financial agreement.

Avoid Loans or Advances A frequently heard comment from deadbeat roommates is this: "I'm a little short this month. If you can cover me, I'll pay you back." Keep track. Insist on repayment by a certain date. Don't let this behavior become a habit in your relationship unless you are prepared to pay the majority of the bills and not feel frustrated in so doing.

Some people have a skewed sense of equity when it comes to paying for mutually shared items. These individuals assume that because the roommate is "better off" than they are—with a bigger salary or richer parents—the roommate should pay more of the bills. Roommate-associated bills should be divided equally whenever possible, and unless an arrangement to the contrary has been established.

Secure Your Valuables Keep your jewelry
and other valuable items secure within your room,
apartment, or house. Don't leave them out where
they might become a temptation to your roommate
or to your roommate's friends. The same goes for
cash. It's easy—even between honest roommates
—for a person to borrow a five and forget to return
it if the money is obviously available for the borrowing.

If you suspect that a roommate may not value
your valuables and may be prone to damaging
them, discarding them inadvertently or purposefully, or diminishing their value in some way, store
the items elsewhere, or don't bring them into the
environment that you are sharing together.

6 ❑ Putting It in Writing

A verbal agreement is a good discussion. A written agreement is truly an agreement.

Consider purchasing a ledger and using it as the basis for your agreement.

The Basic Agreement You may want to jot down areas of agreement, noting in two columns:

You Have Paid (include deposits)	*I Have Paid* (include deposits)
You Are Going to Pay (monthly or weekly)	*I Am Going to Pay* (monthly or weekly)
You Will Do These Chores (with this periodicity)	*I Will Do These Chores* (with this periodicity)
You Have These Off-Limits Rules and Items	*I Have These Off-Limits Rules and Items*

Along the way, list special payments or purchases that are made, and keep track of any borrowing or lending that occurs.

House Rules As a separate entry in the book, identify some house rules that both agree to, such as the way you are going to decide what comes into your house in the way of furniture or artifacts, a curfew time for visitors, or use of certain appliances.

Some of the entries might include these:

- Advance purchase agreement—agreeing to discuss the addition of such items as artifacts, plants, pets, and appliances to your living space prior to their acquisition

- Curfews

- Rules regarding guests

- Dissolution responsibilities—agreeing to financial obligations should one person fail to fulfill the full term of a lease or an agreement

Emergency Plans Identify procedures you intend to follow in case of emergencies, and make certain that both identify key people to call should illness or trouble occur. List the people each would want notified in an emergency, their relationship, their phone numbers, the hospital and doctors of choice, and any medications taken regularly.

Shared Schedules and Numbers Provide basic information such as your office work number(s), your company name and supervisor, your course schedule, your team schedule, and so forth.

This gives you a means of finding each other should an emergency arise. You may want to post a calendar on which each notes events and activities pertinent to rooming together.

Inventory Put in writing the inventory of furniture, books, and appliances in your residence—items that belong to each individual and items that are shared. This is good information to have for insurance purposes (and vital in cases of theft, fire, or loss owing to a natural catastrophe).

Signing Off Consider the compilation of your agreement book something that the two of you do together and that both are willing to sign and date. If you amend your agreement, sign the amendments and date them, too. Having such a book doesn't restrict or inhibit a budding relationship nearly as much as you may think. Rather, it provides a memory to which both can refer in times of dispute, difficulty, or genuine tragedy. Such a document signals to both that the relationship as roommates has limitations, boundaries, and obligations. It opens up a basis for communication and for structuring an efficient, productive, and enjoyable way of living together. It also readily reveals inequities and improper division of labor, responsibility, or payments. Ultimately, it provides a starting point that ideally is a win-win situation for both parties.

Accessibility Keep your ledger or agreement in a place that is readily accessible to both of you.

Multiple Roommates If you have more than one roommate, make certain each person has input into and signs all aspects of the agreement.

7 ❏ Anticipate Moving On

In recognizing the temporary nature of your rooming-together situation, you will likely want to take several very practical measures to ensure a minimum amount of disputes and hurt feelings when the time comes for the two of you to part company.

Inventory As mentioned earlier, keep a running inventory of possessions and a record of who purchases what. You may want to identify certain items with small pieces of masking tape on which you put the owner's initials.

Buying Separately Avoid making joint purchases. Seek to own items individually. If the two of you make a common purchase—a practice that is to be avoided but is occasionally necessary—keep record of how much each person paid toward the item.

Limited Purchases Don't commit yourself to payments for any piece of furniture or appliance that goes beyond the term of your lease or the amount of time you anticipate living in a place with your roommate. Don't buy in massive quantities unless you expect to use the full supply prior to the time of your anticipated departure.

Move-Out Day   Plan to be present on the day that your roommate moves out. It's easier to keep certain items from walking out the door than to get them back later. (Your roommate may very well not be at fault here—rather, a helping friend may unintentionally remove something he thinks belongs to your roommate.)

Sufficient Notice   If you suspect that you will be leaving prior to the time you initially anticipated, let your roommate know as soon as you know. Talk over your decision and what financial, legal, or moral obligations are still outstanding between the two of you. Your leaving—or that of your roommate —should never be a surprise.

8 ❏ Music

If you're into classical, and he's into hard rock, if you're into cha-cha, and she's into saxophone blues, you're on different wavelengths!

Rather than subject your roommate to music that he detests, consider these ideas.

Have Separate Systems   If you have more than one room and have two radios, tape or disc players, or stereo systems, put the systems in separate rooms. That way, you can listen to your sound without offending your roommate. (Keep the noise level down so that each can enjoy the music without bleed-through to another room.)

Use Headphones   Listen to what you want, when you want, by means of headphones. This is also a considerate option for times when your roommate is attempting to sleep or study.

Find a Compromise   Is there a type of music that both enjoy and can agree to listen to when you are together? If so, play that. Save your personal favorite genre for times when you have the room or apartment to yourself.

Turn Off the Sound   Try silence. It's something both people can come to appreciate, especially when study time rolls around or the pressures of life are heavy-duty.

Offer Variety in Entertaining   If friends invade your space, take turns playing disc jockey. Expose your friends to various sounds and artists.

Be Courteous to Neighbors   Remember that your walls do have ears—those of the folks who live on either side of you and those of the people who live upstairs or downstairs. Keep your music confined to your space. Turn off the bass boosters. Be especially sensitive to neighbors who may be sleeping or who may have small children. Your right to listen to your music ends at your neighbor's ear.

9 ❑ Space to Yourself

The busier your schedule, the more friends you have, the fuller your plate of responsibilities and obligations, the more likely that you'll enjoy having space to yourself—a cave into which you can crawl and escape from the outside world. Perhaps nothing is more irksome or frustrating than to realize that someone else is in your cave just when you need most to have it to yourself!

Be sensitive to your roommate's need to have the room or apartment to himself. That need may be for a couple of hours each day, a few hours each week, or an entire day from time to time. At the same time, express your need for some alone-in-the-cave time.

Free Up the Common Space If you share an apartment and have separate bedrooms, periodically go to your own room so that your roommate can have full access to the common living space you share. If you share a room in a house or dorm that has a common lobby, periodically go to the lobby so your roommate can have the room to herself. (Point out what you are doing and give an expected return time so that your roommate will know that she truly has the space to herself for a while. Pointing this out also voices an expectation, of sorts, that you would appreciate the same gesture from time to time.)

Preserve the Privacy of One's Room
Agree with your roommate that if you go to your room and close the door, it is a signal that you want to be alone, quiet, and undisturbed. Let your roommate know if you are available for phone calls or if you prefer total isolation. Always knock before entering a roommate's private space. Make use of "Do Not Disturb" signs.

Find a Private Space Elsewhere   If possible, find a place outside your shared environment where you can go to be alone. It may be a study niche in the library or a place where you can park your car and enjoy an hour of scenic beauty while musing about life and listening to your favorite music.

10 ❏ Time to Yourself

Don't let your roommate fill your entire schedule with his plans or needs.

In addition to the time required by your employer, professors, teammates, lab partners, club colleagues, family members, and friends is the time a roommate will require of you. This will include time spent communicating about and resolving living-space or relationship problems, time spent cleaning your shared environment, time spent hosting mutual friends, and time spent getting better acquainted with each other. Be prepared to spend time with your roommate. Budget for it. Plan for it. Schedule it.

Avoid, however, the tendency of a roommate to schedule all of your uncommitted time. Some individuals are very good at taking advantage of the goodwill or available time of others. Listen closely for patterns of behavior that may be introduced by such phrases as these:

- "If you're not doing anything . . ."
- "Would it be at all possible for you to . . ."
- "As long as you're free right now . . ."

- "I've been waiting for you to come home so we can . . ."

Your unscheduled time is your unscheduled time, not necessarily time available to fulfill the needs or desires of a roommate. You don't need to apologize for not helping your roommate or doing what your roommate wants to do. Simply say, "I may not look busy to you, but I've actually scheduled this time for rest and relaxation. I need a little time to gather my thoughts, sort my feelings, and expand my imagination."

Your Own Schedule Let your roommate know that you aren't responsible for going to functions for which you personally haven't accepted an invitation—in other words, your roommate has no authority to obligate you without your permission or agreement. You should also feel free to let a roommate know that you need advance notice so you can schedule time for shared errand running or chore doing—in other words, you aren't at the beck and call of your roommate's whims about when the freezer needs defrosting or the carpet needs shampooing.

A Shared Living Space, Not Necessarily Shared Lives Make it clear to a roommate who invades your schedule that rooming together implies a sharing of space, not a sharing of lives. Learning how to share space is a necessary component of being roommates. Sharing lives is something that is by invitation only, neither an obligation nor something that is automatically a part of rooming together.

11 ❑ Friends and Parties

In inviting a friend to your room or apartment, always keep in mind that you share that space with someone else. Ask yourself,

- Will my roommate be comfortable walking into our mutually shared space and finding us there?

- Will my roommate be uncomfortable knowing that this person was in our room (or apartment) when he wasn't there?

- How will my roommate feel having us walk in on her (assuming she is at home)?

Don't assume that the answers to these questions are your roommate's problem. It is part of your responsibility as a good roommate to take into consideration the feelings of your roommate prior to doing anything that involves your shared environment. The space you share is not your room or apartment but only partially your room or apartment.

Ask First   When in doubt and whenever possible, ask your roommate in advance of bringing a friend or friends into the environment you share. You may want to agree on friend hours—certain times of a day or week when each has the privilege of inviting others into the shared space without asking permission or giving notice first.

Be Sensitive   Your roommate should never be made to feel uncomfortable in the space he calls home. Don't exclude your roommate from conversations that you are having in a shared living area. Don't ignore your roommate's presence. Don't fail to invite your roommate to a party in his own living room. Don't embarrass your roommate with language or behavior that you know is offensive to him.

Don't assume that your roommate will like your friends as much as you do. Maybe so; maybe not.

Extend Veto Power   Extend to each other veto power on certain people or events in your shared space. It isn't intended as a means of psychological warfare; it is a means of sharing space peacefully. If your roommate doesn't want to cohost the parties you desire to give, host the parties elsewhere. If your roommate doesn't value some of your friends as highly as you do, hang out with them someplace other than your room or apartment. Conversely, you should be able to say to your roommate, "I prefer not to have that person in the apartment (or room)," or "I'd rather our room not be the site of this weekend's bash."

Clarify Host Responsibilities If you do host a friend or party—with your roommate's agreement—bear in mind that you are responsible for that party, including the actions of your friend or guests or any friends of friends who may stop by! You are responsible for cleaning up their messes, repairing their damages, restoring any losses they inflict (including anything they may steal), paying for what they consume (including what they consume of food and beverages copurchased by your roommate), and controlling their behavior within your shared living space. Your roommate is not under any obligation to help you clean up, fix up, or mend wrongs unless she agreed to cohost the event. Your restoration of your shared environment to its original state should be timely.

12 ❑ Daily Chores

Certain chores need to be done on a daily basis for two people to share a space comfortably. Below are twelve rules to consider together as roommates. Some of them don't apply to all situations, but all of them apply to some situations!

1. Put trash in the trash can immediately Don't litter your shared space.

2. Empty the trash daily Keep food odors and bugs away.

3. Wash dishes immediately after their use If you want to leave grimy dishes soaking, consider keeping one part of the sink filled with sudsy water so that dishes can soak out of sight prior to your washing them or loading them in a dishwasher. If you have a garbage disposal, run it each time you put something into it.

4. Make your bed This is especially important if it is in your shared space or if it is readily viewed from a shared space.

5. Pick up your clothes Again, this applies to all shared spaces—including living room, bathroom, or bedroom.

6. Keep the newspaper sections together   Toss the paper after (and only after) it's been read by both parties.

7. Clean up spills and messes as soon as they happen   That includes any messes made by pets or friends.

8. Monitor supplies   If you're running low on a cleaning supply or a shared kitchen or bathroom item (such as dishwasher soap, mayonnaise, or toilet tissue), put it on the shopping list immediately so the supply can be replenished before you are likely to run out completely.

9. Leave a note   When do you expect to be back? How do you want your phone messages answered? Also let your roommate know if you have an unusual daily schedule (so he will know how to find you in an emergency).

10. Let your roommate know your dinner plans   Are you planning dinner at home, planning to bring home a friend, or planning to do anything out of the ordinary routine related to your shared space or schedule?

11. Leave a shared bathroom or kitchen clean and neat   For example, don't leave a ring around the tub, wet towels on the floor, toothpaste in the sink, coffee grinds in the sink, or a puddle of milk on the floor!

12. Update your message board   Remove old messages or items that have been discussed.

Bear in mind that if you can learn to live with a roommate successfully on a daily basis, you have a much better chance at living together successfully for a week, month, term, semester, or year.

13 □ Weekly and Monthly Chores

Just as a shared environment creates daily chores, so other chores and responsibilities tend to pop up weekly or monthly. Here are twelve such chores to consider as you divide responsibilities. This is not a comprehensive list, of course. You and your roommate no doubt will find other things that need to be added or substitutions that need to be made.

1. Vacuum or shampoo carpets Mop or clean hard-surface floors.

2. Clean the bathroom (sink, tub or shower, and toilet)

3. Dust, polish, or clean hard surfaces They include furniture, artifacts, windows, and mirrors.

4. Pay bills

5. Water houseplants

6. Sort out refrigerator Discard all inedibles and unknowables.

7. Do laundry of shared items, such as bathroom rugs and guest towels

8. List and shop for shared consumable items (grocery, sundry, hardware)

9. Make any needed home repairs   Or take items to be repaired professionally.

10. Discard no-longer-usable items   Toss out magazines both have read, withered bouquets, and stacks of unopened junk mail. Don't, however, discard something belonging to your roommate without first getting permission!

11. Go over your schedules together   Make notes related to unusual events or activities in the coming week or month.

12. Update your agreement book   Discuss protocol, inventory, expenses, rules, and so forth.

Rotate chores so that one person doesn't always get stuck doing the same despicable task. Plan your schedules in advance, and whenever possible, clean together. The chores will go faster and be more enjoyable. Talk over mutual issues as you work. You may find it easier to talk out problems if you work as you talk.

14 ❏ Household Curfew

Most dorms, sorority and fraternity houses, camps, barracks, and even some apartment complexes and communities have curfews set by authorities responsible for maintaining order among a group of people. Think of your household curfew as a rule that you and your roommate are privileged to set and define for yourselves for much the same purpose: to maintain orderliness in your life together.

You may define your curfew in a number of ways:

- Lights out—each person might still hold the privilege of resorting to an individual book-reading light or a desk lamp.

- Music off—again, each person might hold out the privilege of resorting to headphones or music played quietly in the confines of an individual room.

- Phone unplugged—give a roommate sharing the same room the privilege of uninterrupted sleep; outgoing calls might be retained as an individual privilege.

- Guests leave—having a space free of guests is especially important if you are sharing only one room or an efficiency apartment with a roommate.

Flexibility   From time to time, you may want to adjust your self-imposed curfew hours—for example, setting them earlier during finals week or later on Saturday nights.

Quiet Zones   You may also want to negotiate the possibility of quiet hours during a day or evening—perhaps a two- or three-hour time block each day when your room becomes off-limits to visitors or the music is turned off.

Setting a curfew with a roommate gives both of you a sense of control over your own space and time within the broader context of your community or school. It's a private ordering of your lives and, in that, an opportunity to have some structured time and space both can count on in the midst of what is likely to be a hectic parade of people and activities.

15 □ Overnight Guests

What's the Problem?   Although this point of negotiation may not seem to exist for many roommates—for example, if overnight guests are forbidden—the issue of overnight guests tends to become an issue for two reasons.

First, and generally speaking, "no overnight guests" rules usually apply only to guests of the opposite sex. Rarely do even the strictest dormitories in the most conservative institutions forbid the camping out of a member of the same sex and community on the floor of your room. From that perspective, consider the case of a mutual friend who for some reason doesn't want to sleep in his own room—owing, for instance, to a fight with his roommate. Consider, as another example, the visitor who just gets too sleepy to walk across campus to her own dorm room or who stays past the lock-in hour and doesn't want to be discovered outside her dormitory.

Second, people are prone to test rules. If "no overnight guests" is a rule, somebody is likely to test the boundaries of that rule "just to see if we can get away with it."

The result: overnight guests are not all that rare!

Cohosts or No Hosts   Apartment dwellers, of course, are likely to encounter many potential overnight guests, from the out-of-town visitor who just happened to drop in at ten o'clock at night to the girlfriend or boyfriend who fell asleep and can't be pried off the sofa.

Perhaps the safest and easiest outlet for both roommates is to establish a household rule: no overnight guests without the permission of *both* roommates. Each person has a say in who stays and who doesn't. This rule gives a timid, peer-pressured host an out in insisting that his own friends leave the room or apartment at an appropriate time. And it gives both roommates the freedom of knowing that if they get up in the middle of the night, they aren't likely to stumble over unknown persons in the room or apartment.

"Utte" Time   To implement this rule, establish with your roommate an ideal "utte" time ("urge them toward exiting"). One set of roommates called this "vamonos time"—taken from the Spanish for "get thee hence." Once that magic hour arrives, you and your roommate might begin to give hints that it's time for all guests to pack up and go. You may want to post a sign on a wall, as one set of roommates did: "No Parking Here After 11:00 P.M."

One good way to establish a "no overnight guests" rule is to declare the last two hours of any day to be a study time. Nearly all guests can relate to that need or desire.

Safe Escort If a guest needs escorting home, do so—leaving in ample time so as to return by your own household curfew.

If a guest needs to have a cab called on his behalf, do so in sufficient time to honor your own curfew.

Hospitality If a guest pleads to stay, saying she has no other place to go, help her find a place. The laws of hospitality do not require that you give shelter to a person overnight—only that you help the person along the journey!

16 □ Temperature

Some like it hotter, some colder. And rarely are both people 100 percent comfortable at all times. Such is the lot of roommates.

Your goal is to keep the thermostat from becoming a war zone.

Find a temperature that both find tolerable. Generally, the cooler temperature desired will be the one both can accommodate since it's easier to pile on blankets or wear sweaters than to strip away garments. Small fans or space heaters can also be a real help in adjusting temperature for personal comfort.

Reduce Bills   Utility bills may well become a factor in deciding just how much heating or air conditioning is going to be done in your space. Don't argue about that outrageously high utility bill that takes both by surprise. Rather, use your own energy to find a way of lowering your bill next month.

Open Up   Do your best to acclimate to the outside temperature and to make good use of open windows as long as your space remains secure and all open windows or doors are screened. To generate a flow of air through a room, you'll need to have an outlet for it, not only an inlet. Perhaps a neighbor across the hall can help you create a breeze tunnel in your dormitory during warm afternoons.

Drape It Use sun-blocking curtains, window shades (perhaps even dark ones), or aluminum panels to keep a room with south- or west-facing windows a few degrees cooler during the heat of a day. Open draperies to give sun plenty of access on winter days (assuming that you have well-sealed windows).

Cool It Use heat-generating appliances (such as ovens and dryers) only in the cool of a summer day.

Seal It The better sealed your room or apartment, the more even the temperature you will be able to maintain. Check for leaks around windows and doors, and plug them up to the best of your ability (and perhaps with some help from your landlord or dorm director).

17 □ Annoying Habits

From the clicking of pens to the grinding of teeth to the popping of gum, annoying habits abound. We all face the problem of coping with the "I just can't take it anymore" behaviors of others. *Expect* your roommate to annoy you, and you won't be disappointed! At the same time, however, expect to be told at some point that something you do is equally irritating to that person!

Be Realistic Ask yourself a simple question before reacting to your roommate: Can this be controlled? Snoring probably can't. On the other hand, hitting the snooze button five times consecutively before rising in the morning (resulting in six blasts of the alarm) can be controlled.

If the problem is one that your roommate can't stop—or even if she willfully chooses not to stop it —prepare yourself to take creative action. Invest in earplugs perhaps. Or get up and turn off the alarm yourself—definitively.

Evaluate Your Response Are you overreacting? Is this something you should ignore? Is it a habit that violates your preestablished agreement? If a habit keeps you from sleep, creates extra work for you, violates your freedom to breathe, move, eat, or otherwise live in your own space, you need to address it. If your roommate's behavior becomes a matter of control for you—that is, you feel an overpowering urgency to stop that person's behavior—weigh your response before confronting your roommate.

Register Your Concern   Don't stuff an ongoing annoyance. It will come out in snide remarks, bitterness, frustration, and perhaps even ulcers. Meanwhile, your roommate will be blissfully ignorant and continue to annoy. Let your roommate know that you'd like to see a change in behavior. Don't accuse. Simply state. Here are some possible opening lines:

- The We're-in-This-Together Approach: "Is there something we can do about . . . [and cite problem]?"

- The Self-on-the-Line Approach: "I know that I have lots of habits that I'm not aware of, and I'd like to know if there's something I do that annoys you." And then after hearing an earful, you can follow up: "Wow! All that. And the only thing that I find annoying is . . . [and cite your foremost peeve]."

- The Direct Approach: "Are you aware that you . . . [and cite habit]?"

- The "Future Good" Approach: "Your spouse someday is probably going to tell you that you . . . [cite annoyance]. Maybe that's why God let me be your roommate—so you can work on that *before* it becomes a marriage problem!"

Be creative. Be kind. But state your case. Little annoyances can build into huge problems. And unless they are dealt with in a positive, constructive way, you may very well develop a habit of denial. Denial is not a minor habit, and it can do more than annoy; it can destroy a relationship of value.

Never ridicule your roommate for a habit he can't control or one he is working to change.

18 □ Pets

Face It No matter how cute, cuddly, or innocuous a pet seems to be at the outset, it becomes a third roommate. Face that fact squarely. Even if the pet belongs to your roommate, it becomes your pet, too, to a certain extent.

Recognize these factors about pets:

- Pets make messes and sometimes cause damage that falls into the category of major repairs.

- Pets make noise—even if it's the drone of the pump in the fish tank.

- Pets require care—full water and food dishes, changed papers or litter boxes, walks in the park, and trips to the vet.

This is not to say no to pets but to raise a strong caution flag. Pets can be lovable and comforting—a good security measure and a source of companionship and even inspiration. But weigh carefully their presence in your space.

Ground Rules   Here are some courtesy rules
to consider:

- Always let a potential roommate know fully
  about your pets before you agree to room
  together.

- Never foist a pet on a roommate who is aller-
  gic to that species or who simply doesn't like
  that species or particular animal.

- Never require that your roommate provide
  care for your pet—including responsibility
  for cleaning up the messes it creates, paying
  for the damage it causes, or feeding it when
  you are away for a weekend.

- Don't bring home a pet without your roommate's full and enthusiastic permission.

- Make certain that one of you owns the pet
  fully. Don't buy a puppy together, and then
  face "pet custody" arguments when the time
  comes for you to part company.

- Keep your pet's food and water containers
  clean. That also applies to the cage, tank, or
  litter box.

- Store items related to your pet in your room,
  not in shared space.

- Do not hold your roommate responsible for
  the disappearance of a free-roaming pet.

- Do not ask your roommate to pet-sit for you.

- Do confine your pet to your personal space (for example, your bedroom) when your roommate is entertaining in shared spaces.

All of this applies, of course, to situations in which you are allowed to keep pets. Most dorms prohibit them.

19 ❑ Sharing Meals

Food is a major factor in life and, therefore, in roommate relationships. To share, or not to share? To eat together, or to eat separately? These are the questions!

Four Approaches   Each is different, but all worked equally well for the parties involved.

1. Both roommates went their separate ways, eating virtually all of their meals outside their apartment
They had separate cupboards and separate shelves in the refrigerator for their beverages and snack items. In a year of living together, they shared only two meals: Chinese take-out.

2. Both roommates ate in the dormitory dining hall and kept a basket of chips, cookies, and popcorn in their room for snacks   They kept the same things on hand at all times and took turns buying their supply on a weekly basis.

3. The roommates went their separate ways for breakfast and lunch, and they shared evening meals together at least five times a week   For the evening meals, they pooled their resources and shopped and cooked together.

4. Both roommates shared a common stash of coffee, fruit, and cereal for breakfast Each roommate agreed to cook two evening meals a week and purchased all items related to that meal on her own. Leftovers from meals were shared mutually for snacks or for lunches. On other nights of the week, they played it by ear—sometimes ordering in a pizza, at other times going out together or separately, and at still other times making their own sandwiches.

Whatever works for you and your roommate works! Talk over your schedules, your food budgets, and your desires related to mealtimes.

Avoid the Pitfalls Here are five courtesy rules that can help eliminate some of the pitfalls roommates frequently encounter in sharing food.

1. Don't eat what you don't pay for If you helped to purchase half of the groceries, expect to eat half of the food—and only half.

2. Don't expect shared food to be there the next time you open the refrigerator

3. Don't count bites In any given period, one person is going to eat a little more from the common pantry than the other.

4. Do take into consideration different eating habits If you are sharing groceries, make sure that your pantry has foods that both enjoy.

5. Do take into consideration different consumption rates   A three-hundred-pound athlete and a ninety-five-pound couch potato will consume different quantities of food. Two people of the same weight may have very different metabolisms. You may want to prorate your contributions toward food expenses according to average consumption rather than divide the bills fifty-fifty.

20 ❑ "Personal" Food

Consider "personal" food to be what you purchase solely, what is a gift to you exclusively, and what you intend for your sole consumption (or the consumption of those you designate—for example, party food for *your* guests).

Do not, in contrast, consider personal food to be what you prepare or what you have a particular fondness for.

Agree with your roommate in advance that personal food items will be personal food items   It doesn't matter how tempting they look, how noble the intention of replacing what is eaten, and how hungry one of you may be!

Label personal food items as "personal" or put your name on them   If you don't want a roommate nibbling on the pie you stored on the common shelf in the refrigerator, label it, "Don't touch! For tomorrow's open house!"

Purchase personal items separately   Don't segregate jointly purchased items and claim them as your own.

Do keep personal food items covered or out of sight, if possible, to avoid openly tempting your roommate or her friends   Some people assume that they have the privilege to consume whatever they find in another person's refrigerator or cupboards. If that's not the accepted behavior in your haven, do your best to keep especially wonderful treats out of sight.

Don't expect standard supplies to be personal   It may be a nice idea, but it's an unrealistic practice. Expect such items as mayonnaise, ketchup, tea, coffee, mustard, salad dressing, and so forth to be shared items.

Have an understanding with your roommate: you don't raid my care package from home, and I won't raid yours. On the other hand, generosity pays off. Giving your roommate a piece of the lemon bundt cake your grandmother sends from Iowa City may keep him from demolishing the entire cake!

21 ❑ Shopping

Designated Shopper Decide between you who is going to shop and for what. A simple system that seems to work for a number of roommates is this:

- Keep a running list of shared items that need to be purchased.

- Estimate how much the items are going to cost.

- Designate a shopper.

- Each person chips in half of what the bill will likely be and agrees to cover half of any overage (or receive half of any change).

At the outset, you may want to shop together. You'll probably find that one of you enjoys shopping more and has a better eye for bargains. If that's the case, let that person do the shopping. You may want to trade off that chore by undertaking an additional one on the home front (such as doing the dishes). Or you may want to trade off shopping responsibilities as your schedules allow.

How Much for What? Decide what level of quality you intend to purchase. A person with a meager food budget may discover that she has left the shopping up to a roommate with gourmet tastes! If you put beef on your list, agree in advance about whether that means filet mignon or hamburger.

Stick to the List If you have made a list together, agree that jointly made purchases will include only what's on the list—regardless of the "great buy" or "too delicious to pass up" item that the designated shopper spies.

Receipt Jar Another system that has worked for several sets of roommates is the receipt jar. Each roommate purchases shared food items (from a shopping list) and then puts the receipt for the purchase in a small jar in the kitchen. The receipt is labeled first with the name of the person who paid. (Receipts for all shared expenses—items such as home delivery of newspapers, utility bills, and service charges—also go into the jar.) At the end of the month, the receipts are totaled and split in half. Individual totals are prepared for each person, and the difference is paid to the party who spent more.

Separate Checks If you are doing personal shopping at the same time you are shopping for your jointly shared sundries or food, segregate your purchases and have the checker give you two receipts. You'll save yourself a math problem.

22 ❑ Separate Wardrobes

No matter how good a friend your roommate is or how much you want to wear an item, don't borrow your roommate's clothing without specific permission. Even then, recognize that clothes sharing is not a very good idea.

Responsible Borrowing If your roommate does agree, however, that you may wear an item or outfit, keep in mind that you are responsible for

- cleaning it—either washing it or dry cleaning it, and making sure that it is restored to the closet in a ready-to-wear manner (starched, ironed, folded or hung).

- mending it or repairing it if you have caused any damage to the garment. If you are not capable of mending the garment yourself, you are responsible for getting it professionally repaired.

- replacing it if you damage it beyond repair, lose it, or stain it so that it can't be cleaned.

In addition to being responsible for the garment while you have it in your possession, you are responsible for it while it is being cleaned or repaired.

Shoes and Accessories What applies to items of clothing also applies to jewelry, shoes, purses, ties, scarves, belts, undergarments, and any other accessory items.

Borrowing without permission is a form of theft and deceit, regardless of your intentions or motivations.

Buying Together Some roommates have been known to purchase an outfit together, a practice that is rarely wise. Still, one set of roommates —who shared a room for a summer-long internship that required they wear ties—purchased four ties together, which they rotated and wore alternately. At summer's end, they divided the ties between them—two each—and returned to their respective schools and their wardrobes of jeans and T-shirts. Sharing garments can work, but always within limits and always if it is the result of a mutual agreement.

23 ❏ Avoid Buying Together

The great temptation of new apartment-dwelling roommates or penny-poor college roomies is to buy appliances or furniture together. As in the case of clothes, that rarely turns out to be a good idea. Avoid buying it together if at all possible. If you must purchase an item together in order to have a fridge in the kitchen or a chair in the living room, consider these points.

Receipts Keep the original receipt, and post it or staple it into your agreement book. Mark on the receipt or in your ledger who paid for the item and how it was paid for (check number, credit card number).

Buyout Option Whenever possible, have one person buy out the other as quickly as possible so that each major item has only one owner.

For example, assume that the two of you would like to purchase a small refrigerator for your room —something you find for $129 on sale at a local discount house. If both put in $65, keep track of that investment, and if at all possible, have one person pay the other $65 so that ownership resides with just one person. Or should both of you decide you want a small chair that you find at a garage sale and the price of that is $65, have one person buy it and give it to the other person as payment. (The first person ends up owning the fridge and the other person the chair.) This method keeps you from reaching the end of a roommate relationship with each of you owning half of a wide variety of used appliances and furniture (some items that neither may want and other items that both may want)!

Equal at Parting Even though the items you purchase will be in various degrees of the "used" category by the time you part company, consider division of property to be on a fifty-fifty basis based on the original purchase price of items. Total all the items you have purchased, and divide the sum in half. Divide items according to who purchased what until you come as close as possible to the half-and-half point, and then have the person who is long on goods equalize the balance sheet with a cash payment to the person who is short.

24 ❑ Communicat- ing

Take time to talk to your roommate—not just about the grocery list, the piled-up trash in the entry, or your daily schedule but about your lives. Get to know the person with whom you are sharing space and goods. Even if you don't become close friends, you'll know better the motivations, trigger points, and feelings of your roommate, which can help you become a more understanding and easy-to-live-with companion.

Here are some suggestions for enhancing your communication.

Make time to talk to your roommate Any relationship deteriorates without communication, even that between the most casual and uncommitted roommates. Don't simply toss sentences at each other as you pass in the hall. Sit down and share a meal or two together each week. Allow time for conversation. Make yourself available to listen to your roommate. It doesn't mean you need to become embroiled in all of his problems; it does mean you should extend to your roommate the basic courtesy of being a caring human being.

Don't "fall silent" without an explanation   Don't use silence as a weapon or as a punishment of your roommate. If you are annoyed about something or have a concern related to your living quarters or your relationship, speak up. Issues that ferment in silence tend to explode in anger rather than in reasonable problem-solving discussion.

If your concern about studies, romance, job, family, or another personal issue causes you to feel depressed or melancholy, let your roommate know why you are suddenly moping about in silence. Otherwise, your roommate is likely to assume your mood is the result of something she has done. Your roommate can't read your mind; let her know what is bothering you or why you are silent.

Write notes   Provide as many details as you can in relaying phone messages to your roommate. Leave a note letting your roommate know where you are or when you will be back—especially if he is expecting you to be at a different place or to arrive at a certain time. Put amounts and lists into writing rather than rely on oral communication to remind your roommate to purchase laundry detergent or pay you for half of the phone bill.

Keep your roommate's secrets   Consider your relationship with your roommate to be confidential. Don't spread gossip about your roommate. Don't tell her secrets. Don't relay her hopes or dreams. And don't complain about your roommate's habits or behavior to others; if you have a problem, work it out between the two of you.

25 □ Leading Separate Lives

Sharing the same space does not mean that you and your roommate must lead the same life. You and your roommate have separate identities, unique tastes and preferences, individual schedules and, in many cases, completely different circles of friends.

Don't expect your roommate to believe what you believe, hold the opinion you hold, like the activities you enjoy, laugh at the same jokes that tickle your fancy, see what you see in your friends, like the foods you enjoy eating, listen to the music or watch the television programs that you choose, or appreciate the same things in life!

And that's okay!

Your roommate is not a spouse or an automatic best friend. Your roommate is not necessarily a kindred spirit. In fact, you may not even choose to spend much time with your roommate.

Mutuality If friendship develops, great. If you find that you and your roommate have common interests, all the better. But don't dismiss the value of your roommate because you don't seem to have anything in common. Commonality and mutuality are two different things. Roommates can have mutual responsibility for a mutually shared space while holding very little in common on a personal level.

Expectations Roommates tend to expect one of two things from each other, especially in situations where they are preassigned or are unfamiliar with each other prior to their rooming together. Both expectations tend to be extreme:

- Each expects the other to be a built-in buddy —a person with whom to go places, eat meals, and spend time. A roommate, from this perspective, tends to be taken for granted—he becomes the person who is always there if nobody else is available. *Don't* take your roommate for granted. Spend some time cultivating your relationship with him as a first priority!

- Each expects no association, regarding the situation as that of two ships docked in the same port. *Do* expect to have a relationship with your roommate—to learn something from her, to communicate with her, and to negotiate time, space, and responsibilities with her.

Balance The key here is balance. You do, should, and can have a relationship with your roommate. That relationship, however, is subject to definition, negotiation, and development. It will become what the two of you want it to become. You alone can't determine what your roommate will be to you or how much of your lives will overlap; neither is that choice up to your roommate. It is something you must work on together.

Perhaps the wisest approach to take is this: plan to walk separate paths, but continually look for places where you might intersect or merge your energies, interests, or affiliations.

26 ❑ Respect Each Other's Property

Perhaps nothing strains a roommate relationship more rapidly and more intensely than suspecting that your roommate is mistreating your property or using your things without getting permission first. Nothing raises defenses or caution signs more readily, and few things are resented more.

Stealing is broadly defined as "taking something that does not rightfully belong to you." It may be just a squirt of hair spray, a pen that never makes it back to your roommate's desk, or a bite of your roommate's personal food that you hope will go unnoticed. However small or insignificant the item, the fact remains: you have taken something that wasn't yours.

Borrowing May Be Stealing in Disguise

Stealing may be using a piece of your roommate's luggage that you were sure your roommate didn't need over the weekend, borrowing a book that you just wanted to consult for the evening (and that you forgot to bring back from the library), or grabbing an umbrella (which you assumed your roommate wouldn't need since you also assumed your roommate wouldn't be going out).

Stealing includes availing yourself of information, opinions, or research that weren't of your own creation—for example, copying study notes, plagiarizing papers, or lifting original ideas that you may have discussed and that somehow find their way into your paper or test essay.

Make Amends   If you have taken from your roommate, admit what you have done (to yourself and to your roommate), make restitution if at all possible (restoring what has been taken and resupplying what has been used), and resolve within yourself to turn over a new leaf and stick solely to what is rightfully yours.

27 ❑ Appreciating Differences

Consider these three unlikely matchups as roommates.

The Differences Paul was into sports, playing on virtually every intramural team sponsored by his dorm and watching all the major games on television. He had an active social life and was an avid phone friend to many. Bill, his roommate, was into academics—a premedicine biology major. He spent most of his free time attending jazz concerts and hanging out at a nearby café with other premed majors.

Marie was more into clothes, men, and her job at the deli than into her classes at college. Her roommate Joycelyn was engaged to be married, liked to stay at home and entertain simply, and was an avid churchgoer.

Casey was a grad student carrying a full course load who also worked thirty-five hours a week as a secretary at the university. She had little free time, and most of her friends were fellow students. Kambra was a foreign student who had dropped out of college, was working full-time as a secretary, and was seriously involved romantically with another foreign student and had virtually no other friends.

Disasters? Not so. Each set of roommates got along very well and developed friendships that still continue, years after their stints of rooming together.

Willingness to Learn   Paul taught Bill the rules of ice hockey and how to play tennis, and he broadened Bill's musical tastes to include country music. Bill helped Paul see value in studying, introduced him to jazz, and helped him focus on a major field of study.

Marie taught Joycelyn about applying makeup and assembling a wardrobe; Joycelyn taught Marie how to cook. Both were open to sharing deep feelings and found that, at heart, they had many of the same fears, hopes, and dreams.

Casey learned to speak a foreign language, and Kambra reenrolled as a student. They found they enjoyed giving parties together.

Appreciation and Accommodation   In all three relationships, the roommates learned to appreciate their differences, and they worked hard to find ways to accommodate their differences and turn them into valuable learning experiences.

28 ❑ Applauding Successes

If your roommate does well, applaud her.

If your roommate falls in love, be happy for him.

If your roommate wins the prize, say hooray!

Become an avid member of your roommate's fan club. In so doing, you will generate goodwill between the two of you, and you will grow as a person.

Avoiding Jealousy Many people experience an innate, usually unconscious, desire to compete with their roommates. The competition may be for grades, friends, dates, memberships, and/or recognition. This drive toward competition may very well be a holdover from sibling rivalry, but whatever the underlying motivation, the outcome is usually the creation of an environment in which jealousy takes root very easily.

Once jealousy has taken hold, it tends to yield very ugly fruit: snide remarks, petty sniping, withheld information, bursts of anger and frustration, and even blatant attempts at undermining the other person's opportunities for success. Rather than develop a relationship in which they might become friends, such roommates set themselves toward becoming enemies. The result is usually disastrous, unless at some point there are both open recognition of the competition and mutual apologizing and amends making.

Living with someone who is secretly trying to diminish your ability to succeed is uncomfortable, but it's more uncomfortable living with someone who is openly trying to do so.

Being a Fan   The way to avert jealousy and destroy its bitter fruit is to consciously choose to be your roommate's ally and fan. See your roommate's success as something positive. Encourage her to do her best, to go for the top, to study hard, to be all she can be!

Let others know when your roommate wins or does well. Perhaps even give a party to celebrate his achievement. He'll appreciate your sincere applause, and those who witness your enthusiastic kindness will tend to think more highly of you as a person, too.

It takes a bighearted person to delight in the accomplishments of others. Being bighearted, of course, is a genuine accomplishment in itself—not to mention the fact that bighearted people tend to attract a great many friends!

29 □ The Three C's

A number of problems between roommates can be avoided by following the three C's: consideration, courtesy, and caring.

Consideration Before doing anything that relates to your shared space—whether hanging a poster on the wall or inviting a friend over for dinner—consider the impact of your action on your roommate. Will it cramp his mobility or access to your shared living space? Is it something she will enjoy living with? The best rule of thumb is to ask first.

Seek your roommate's opinion. Defer to his dislikes. Find points of agreement rather than demand your own way. (You can always hang the poster in your closet or go out to eat with your friend if your roommate would rather not have dinner company.)

Courtesy Treat your roommate as you would like to be treated. Speak to your roommate in a kind tone of voice—neither strident nor smarmy. Say "please" and "thank you." Make requests, not demands.

And as much as possible, stay out of your roommate's way—literally. Don't litter shared space with your clothes, books, food wrappers, or discards. Don't spread yourself over the entire room or apartment. Give your roommate space of her own and access to clean and tidy shared space.

Don't hijack the phone, sound waves (with your choice of music usually), or television (insisting always on your favorite programs). Don't take possession of any area of shared space—be it deck, table, desk, chair, sofa, kitchen, or bathtub—to the point that your roommate never or rarely benefits from it.

Caring Be sensitive to the times when your roommate is dog tired, highly irritable, overly stressed, under pressure, extremely busy, or overly committed, or the times when she is experiencing a broken heart, extreme disappointment, financial woes, or homesickness. Listen to her story. And then listen some more. Lend a shoulder to cry on, or give a pat on the back. Find something downright nice to do for your roommate to help ease his pain or workload. Value your roommate by appreciating who he is and saying so. Always uphold your roommate's dignity.

The three *C*'s go a long way toward establishing a relationship that is mutually beneficial and comfortable to come home to.

30 ❑ Talking It Out

Every relationship has points of disagreement, disappointment, or dispute—times and situations in which two lives don't mesh together and one or both parties are uncomfortable, angry, hurt, or confused.

When those times arise—and especially if you see a pattern of behavior developing that you find offensive—seek to resolve the problem with your roommate as quickly as possible.

Optimize Timing Seek a time when both are physically rested and are willing to enter a discussion seriously, soberly, and rationally. Consider the advantages of making an appointment. An appointment says that the problem is a serious one in your opinion and that you want your roommate to have time to think about the problem and work toward a solution in a rational, objective manner. You don't want to enter a shouting match or engage in an emotion-laden argument that creates only more problems between you.

State the problem in advance of your discussion, and give your roommate some time to think things over and suggest a solution. Don't say, "We need to talk," and then fail to tell your roommate the topic. Use that same time between voicing your concern and having a discussion about the problem to do your own thinking, soul-searching, and solution mapping.

Never attempt to resolve a difference if your roommate is under the influence of chemicals, is physically exhausted, or is under extreme emotional pressure.

Have a One-Issue Agenda   Keep your discussion to one pattern of behavior. Work from a written agenda or a written set of notes. Write down your complaint or what you perceive to be the essence of the difficulty. Cite specific examples. Write down what you would like to see as a solution.

Don't threaten or accuse your roommate. Don't attempt to second-guess your roommate's motives or psychoanalyze your roommate's behavior. Don't stray from your central purpose: to resolve the specific problem. Stick to facts and provable evidence related to patterns of behavior, not an unusual isolated instance.

State Your Discomfort   Let your roommate know specifically what concerns you and why. Tell your roommate how you feel. Don't apologize for your feelings or your reaction, and don't threaten your roommate with "change, or I'll . . ." statements. Insist, however, that some compromise or new ground be found between you. At the same

time, don't expect your roommate to agree with you completely. Rather, seek understanding and a means of resolving the problem that allows both of you freedom of expression and a degree of comfort. In other words, seek a win-win situation.

If your roommate is unable to reach a resolution with you during your initial discussion about a problem, ask if he would like to think about it further and discuss the matter again at a later date, or perhaps call in a mediator. Give your roommate the option here. If he neither wants to discuss the problem nor resolve it, seek outside counsel on your own about what you might do to cope with the situation or bring closure to the relationship.

Move Forward   Once a resolution has been made, bury the issue and move forward. Don't sulk or pout. Don't bring up the problem again in an accusatory or belittling way. Do expect your compromise to be put into effect.

31 ❑ Calling In a Mediator

If you reach an impasse with your roommate, call in a mediator.

Your Choice of Mediator In choosing a mediator,

- find someone with whom both are comfortable.

- find someone who has recognized ability or authority in the area in which you have a concern.

- find someone who is in a neutral relationship to both.

Such a mediator may be a peer counselor (but not a personal friend of yours or your roommate's), a resident advisor, a chaplain, a teacher, or a parent (but not yours or your roommate's).

A mediator is not a judge and should not be asked to judge. A dorm director, for example, is not a good person to call in as a mediator if you wish to resolve an issue that relates to your roommate's repeated violation of dorm rules! The dorm director is going to feel the need to judge the situation and mete out punishment.

Refrain from the tendency to beat up on the mediator. As in many cases of domestic violence, roommates who disagree sometimes gang up on the very person that they have sought out as a mediator.

Your mediation session may not be a formal appointment in a counselor's office. It may be quite informal—having a mutually admired person stop by your room to hear both sides of your story and give you advice over a cup of tea at midnight.

Prior to Mediation Reach an agreement that you will abide by the counsel of the mediator you have agreed to consult. That's a vital requirement for mediation to work. Also keep in mind that mediation is likely to be the last step prior to your seeking dissolution of your relationship or your making an appeal to someone who has the authority to require behavior from one or both of you. Thus, mediation is something both must be willing to seek and follow in an attempt to remain roommates. Mediation is based solely on your attempt to resolve a problem and move forward in your relationship. If either you or your roommate does not value your rooming-together situation highly enough to want it to continue, you are wasting your time calling in a mediator.

32 □ Your Right to Choose

The Positives Whenever possible, choose your roommate. You'll benefit in several ways.

You won't feel as if the person has been foisted on you You won't feel that you must endure an incompatible relationship for better or worse because an authority figure has prearranged your life. In other words, you are less likely to experience anger with the system that put the two of you together as roommates.

You'll probably be able to find a person with whom you share some interests, have some degree of mutuality, or have some evidence of compatibility The better you know yourself—what you can live with and what irritates you into near madness—the better you'll be able to discern whether a person is someone with whom you may be able to live in peace.

You'll probably have a chance to discuss some of the agreement aspects of your relationship in advance of actually living together You will have an opportunity to see how well you can communicate with the person, how open both are to compromising and negotiating, and how similar your schedules, tastes, and styles of living are.

With choice, of course, comes responsibility. In choosing a roommate, you may feel more obligated to make the relationship work (which can be good) or more constrained to endure a poor relationship (which can be bad) to validate your choice to others. If you find that you have made a wrong choice, make a new choice to part company and choose again.

Active Choosing Don't go with the flow of an invitation from someone else who casually says to you, "Wanna be roommates?" Give the situation serious thought. Ask yourself, and perhaps the other person, some questions. Take a little time to get to know the person. Actively choose to enter into a roommate relationship. Otherwise, you may regret your decision later or even feel manipulated.

More Than One Choice Some people are so popular that they have several acquaintances or friends who desire to be their roommates. If that's the case with you, consider yourself privileged, but also take the situation seriously. Weigh what you might learn or experience by rooming with each person. Think through—as accurately and objectively as possible, based on your observations and facts—what it might be like to live with the person. The person who on the surface appears to be the most fun may not be the easiest person to live with.

In turning down invitations from those who desire to room with you, be kind and straightforward. You don't need to explain your decision or make apologies for it. The simplest answer is the best: "I'm going to be rooming with _____." If someone asks you to room with her and you don't feel prepared to make an on-the-spot answer, you can always say, "Let's think on that a while."

Facing a Turndown Should you ask someone to room with you only to be rejected, take his decision at face value, and don't read too much into it. He may have been asked by somebody else first, may not feel you'd be compatible, may want to live alone, or may not feel he knows you well enough. If that's the case, he is probably right! Being turned down as a roommate doesn't mean that you wouldn't have been a good roommate or that the person can't continue to be your acquaintance or friend. It simply means that at this time in your lives, rooming together isn't going to be a reality. Ask someone else.

33 ❑ Honesty and Trustworthiness

Perhaps the foremost traits to look for in a roommate are honesty and trustworthiness. Ask yourself, Can I really *trust* this person? Does this person deal with me in an honest and truthful way?

Think About It   Here are some related questions to ask yourself:

- Can I trust the person to keep my confidences? Does he spread gossip? Does he speak well of me behind my back?

- Can I trust this person not to steal from me?

- Can I trust this person to give me solid feedback and straight answers to questions? Does she give me reliable, accurate information? Does she see the world realistically, or do her feelings, fears, or personal illusions cloud her objectivity?

- Can I trust this person to be true to his word and uphold his end of whatever agreement we make?

- Can I trust this person to transact business in an honest, straightforward manner? Am I willing to trust this person with my goods or to spend my money wisely on my behalf?

Other Traits Honesty and trustworthiness are traits that imply a certain degree of openness and a willingness to disclose oneself and to communicate feelings. Do you ever associate your potential roommates with the words *secretive, sneaky,* or *mysterious?* What has led you to make that association? Such persons may be intriguing, but the real question is, Do you want to live with a person who exhibits such behavior toward you?

Do you ever have a feeling that the person is manipulative or that she is a user of people? If so, she probably isn't tremendously trustworthy since such a person usually has a tendency to twist things to her own advantage, sometimes without any regard to the truth.

Look for a roommate who means yes when he says yes and no when he says no. Look for someone who will be forthright in communicating feelings and opinions.

34 ❑ An Ability to Pay

From a very practical standpoint, you need a roommate who can pay for half of the expenses incurred together.

Make a Budget Your first step in evaluating the financial solvency of a rooming-together situation is determining exactly what your expenses are going to be. If you are rooming together in a dorm, your shared expenses may be very minimal—perhaps a can of room freshener and a dust rag. (Some roommates have been known to live together an entire year without any mutual expenses related to the room!) Make a list, including input from your potential roommate, about what you anticipate as shared expenses:

- Rent

- Utilities and basic phone service

- Food

- Home-related supplies (and possibly services, such as renter's insurance)

Decide what percentage of shared expenses each is going to pay—usually fifty-fifty. Stare long and hard at the amount you will owe each week, month, and quarter. Can you pay this readily and still have sufficient funds for your personal expenses? Can your potential roommate pay his part?

Determine Financial Viability   Ask yourself—and even discuss openly with a potential roommate—two key questions related to your roommate's ability to pay.

1. What is this person's source of income?   You don't need to know all the details about a person's income, but you do need to know that your roommate has a source of income (in other words, a job or a regular stipend or allowance), that the income source is steady and reliable, and that the person is capable of paying his share.

2. Does the person handle money well?   Again, you don't need lots of details. Watch for some of these telltale signs, or ask the person directly:

- Does she have a lot of debt? (Does she have credit cards? Are they maxed out?)

- Does he routinely ask for more money (from parents perhaps), advances, or loans?

- Is she quick to repay loans?

- Does he attempt to shirk away from paying his fair share (for example, expecting others always to pick up the tab or cover the check)?

- Does she have the ability to say no to something (a purchase, an activity) because she can't afford it?

- Does he know some of the basics about how to balance a checkbook or how to make and live within a budget?

Be Up-front About Money   Have an understanding with your roommate in advance of your rooming together that you expect and are willing to commit personally to

- prompt payment of mutual expenses. In other words, if the rent is due on the first day of the month, both will pay on the first.

- no requests for money—including loans, advances, or cash to cover personal expenses.

- not leaving the other person with debt that is mutual at the time you part ways.

Establish Collateral   Ask yourself if there is a source to which you can appeal if your roommate fails to pay his part of the expenses. Does he have collateral to which you can lay claim? If your roommate is being supported solely by her parents, are the parents in agreement with your rooming together? Are they prepared to cover your roommate's expenses if she becomes unable to do so?

Have an Emergency Fund People lose jobs. Situations change. Unfortunately, leases and utility bills go on. You may want to insist that your roommate and you put aside a certain amount of money (paying into a fund monthly or in advance of your rooming together) to cover a month's worth of shared expenses so that even in case of emergencies or trouble, you will have time to regroup, give required notice, or find a new source of income.

35 ❑ Cleanliness and Orderliness

The issue of cleanliness and orderliness is relational, not absolute. You don't need to insist that a roommate be a neatnik. You do, however, need to find a roommate who has your same degree of concern about cleanliness and orderliness.

If you don't care what your room or apartment looks like, or how much gunk sticks to your shoes when you walk across the carpet, a roommate who is a slob will be acceptable to you.

On the other hand, if you require that every piece of lint be picked up and that your shared space be picture perfect twenty-four hours a day, a roommate who is anything less than a perfectionist will be unacceptable to you.

Most people fall someplace in between. They have a tolerance for some mess but place limits on how much clutter or dirt is too much. Find someone who has your same basic understanding of what needs to be cleaned and how often. One of the easiest ways to get to this issue of compatibility is to make a cleaning schedule together prior to your rooming together, dividing chores and putting them on a timetable. If your potential roommate doesn't see some chores as necessary or sees far less need to clean than you do, take note! You may be the next odd couple.

Clean and Neat?   Also be sensitive to these issues:

- Is your potential roommate a clean person? Does he bathe daily, wear clean clothes, wash his hair regularly, and have clean nails?

- Does your roommate know how to clean? Can she vacuum a rug or mop a floor? Some people grow up never having to do their own laundry or do any housecleaning chores. Your roommate may be willing to clean but may not know how. Are you prepared to teach?

- Does the person pick up after himself, or does he leave a trail behind him of socks, shoes, ties, magazines and newspapers, and dirty dishes?

How do you feel about the answers to the above questions? Can you tolerate this behavior on a day-in, day-out, month-in, month-out basis?

Cleanliness and Orderliness Differ
Cleanliness refers to actual dirt, grime, spills, waste, and general filth. Orderliness refers to appearance—whether things are in place and the space is visually and aesthetically pleasing. Some people can tolerate a great deal of dirt if the visual

impact is orderly; others can tolerate a great deal of disorganization as long as things are clean. Discuss these issues of cleanliness versus orderliness before you begin rooming with someone.

Perhaps the most obvious way to determine if you are compatible in this area is to visit—unannounced—your potential roommate's current living quarters. And then ask yourself, Could I live in the space that I found?

36 ❑ Compatible Schedules

An important question to ask a potential roommate is, "What's your average day like?"

Routines Listen closely to how the person describes an average day's routine, especially noting the following times.

Sleep and awake times Is your potential roommate a night person? An early morning person? If you are on vastly different schedules, will that suit you? Can you cope with a singing tea kettle at 6:00 A.M. when you normally go to bed at 4:00 A.M.? Will you enjoy coming home to a darkened apartment at noon because your roommate works the night shift and needs to sleep at that time?

Eating times Does your potential roommate regularly eat at 5:00 P.M. in order to spend a long evening studying, and then take a snack break at 11:00 P.M.? How does that compare to your desire to have a good evening meal at 7:00?

Work and quiet times Does the person tend to party until midnight and then study until 3:00 A.M.? If so, can you adjust to that schedule when your norm is to study until midnight and then go out for an hour of coffee and conversation before bedtime?

Weekends Ask your potential roommate how she spends her weekends. If Saturday mornings don't exist for her because she's catching up on sleep, and that's the time you normally love to clean house, you may have a serious problem! Does your roommate go away every weekend? Does that mean you'll be left with all the household chores?

Roommates obviously do not need to have identical schedules, and even vast differences can be accommodated. But you are wise to discover and talk about your differences in schedules before you start rooming together. Generally speaking, day people should seek to room with day people and night people with night people. If you plan to share meals, you need to settle on a mealtime that works for both. And ultimately, both need to have social and alone time as well as quiet hours that allow rest or study. The greater your initial differences in schedules, the more likely the need to compromise and negotiate.

37 ❑ Addictions

If you are considering rooming with a person who uses illegal drugs, don't. Not only will you be subject to various legal problems (including the possibility of possession charges should your shared space be raided by the police), but you will be opening yourself to a host of other problems that inevitably will drain you emotionally and perhaps even financially and materially.

Agree with your potential roommate in advance that your room or apartment will be a drug-free zone. And insist that it stay that way.

Alcohol Are you considering a roommate who is a heavy or habitual drinker? Think long and hard about the realities. Think about the abusive or incoherent behavior that is usually manifested at some point by a heavy drinker. Think about living with a roommate who has habitual hangovers. Think about cleaning up the physical mess that nearly always results from drinking parties. Is the person attempting to numb deep personal pain with alcohol? The problems will affect your relationship, even if the alcohol consumption is kept under control.

Smoking   Smokers and nonsmokers can room together, but they generally find it difficult. Smokers resent the fact that they don't always feel free to smoke when and where they want, and that nonsmokers rarely understand their addiction. Nonsmokers resent the smell that creeps into their clothing and furniture, the unemptied ash containers, and the secondhand smoke.

Pills   Are you considering rooming with a person who uses pills—tranquilizers, sleeping pills, painkillers, various kinds of downers and uppers—outside a physician's recommendation just to get through a heavy work or study schedule? Talk it over. The person may very well be addicted to chemicals, even prescriptions. The person who habitually uses pills nearly always exhibits wide mood swings that may be very confusing or frustrating to you as a roommate.

Recovering Addicts   If you are a recovering addict, do not room with a person who is using what you found addictive. If your roommate is a recovering addict, you do not want to be the source of temptation, and you should refrain from having liquor, tobacco, or a well-stocked medicine cabinet as part of your shared residence.

38 ❑ Health Problems

If you or your roommate has a serious health problem or physical disability, recognize that this will affect your relationship in emotional and practical ways. Discuss very openly

- any limitations you have. Do either of you have mobility constraints? Does your living space need to be adjusted to accommodate an inability to reach top shelves or stoop over to open low cabinet doors? Do you need special bathing or toilet accessories?

- the degree of help needed from others. Are you counting on a roommate to help you in some way? Do you anticipate that your roommate will need your help? Does one of you have limitations in running errands or doing routine chores? If you or your roommate is receiving periodic treatment, such as chemotherapy, do you anticipate certain periods in which special kinds of help might be needed?

- emergencies that may arise. Are you a diabetic who may need a roommate to administer an insulin shot or locate a glucose tablet for you in an emergency? Is your roommate a person with epilepsy who may need your assistance during a seizure?

Mental and Emotional Limitations Discuss openly any learning disabilities that you have or your roommate has. A person with learning disabilities may need extreme quiet, for example, to be able to concentrate.

If you or your roommate has been under care for depression, anxiety attacks, or some form of mental or emotional illness, talk over as much as you feel you can about that experience. If you are currently in therapy, you should give your roommate the name of your therapist, even if you don't feel you can divulge all of the details related to the issues you are addressing.

Eating and Sleeping Disorders A person will sometimes find that a roommate is struggling with anorexia or bulimia, sleepwalking or another form of sleep disorder, or hypoglycemia. Discuss ways in which these problems might affect your sharing of food and space.

Injury or Illness The occasional bout with the flu, a broken bone, or a sprained limb will also affect your living situation. Ask these two key questions:

- What do you need for me to do for you?

- What is it that you do not want me to do?

Your roommate may desire your help in taking a note to a teacher or getting a tray from the cafeteria, for example, but may not want you to hover over her when she'd rather sleep in peace.

In rooming with a person, you are not necessarily signing on to be that person's conscience, nurse, alter ego, maid, or health administrator. If you are the person with the incapacity, don't expect a roommate to nag you into doing what you need to do, to wait on you hand and foot, or to lie on your behalf. At the same time, recognize that you need to let your roommate know clearly what you can and cannot do for yourself. Set boundaries for your privacy. Take responsibility for your condition.

Exchange Vital Information   Regardless of your incoming health situation, it's a good idea to exchange names and phone numbers of doctors and hospitals of choice with a roommate. Also provide insurance information and names and numbers of people who need to be notified in an emergency.

Help Each Other Stay Healthy   Learn as much as you can about how to live in good health, and help each other when it comes to eating, exercising, sleeping, and avoiding health hazards.

39 ❏ An Ability to Give and Receive

Roommates need to be good givers and receivers. This ability is at the root of all negotiating and compromising.

Giving Is the person you are considering as a roommate generous? Generosity doesn't have to do with the size of a gift as much as the willingness to give, the frequency of giving, and the spirit of love that motivates the giving.

- Does your roommate extend himself to help others—whether opening doors for the person laden with bundles or showing a person how to work a math problem he doesn't understand?

- Is your potential roommate quick to volunteer? Is she already involved in some form of community service or committed assistance to an individual?

- Does the person share or offer quickly a blanket to a person who is cold or a drink to a person who is thirsty? Is the person hospitable to guests?

- Is the person quick to give compliments or to applaud the success or effort of another?

- Does the person look for a response to his giving—an expected return or reciprocity? Does he talk continually about his giving? (If so, his giving may be an attempt to manipulate or to gain approval.)

Receiving   Is the person you are considering as a roommate capable of receiving a compliment? Does she expect gifts or applause as her due? Does she value gifts given to her? Is she generally appreciative for the things she has? Is she thankful for loving friendships and family members? Does she continually complain about never having enough or about how she has been shortchanged in the supply of things that she has?

A Family Snapshot   Perhaps the best insight into your potential roommate's ability to give and to receive comes from viewing his interaction with his family members. Is he generous in giving to his family, or does he expect solely to receive from them continually? Does he begrudge what his parents give to his siblings? Is he jealous of the attention given to or the success achieved by brothers and sisters? Is he grateful for his family's gifts to him?

Rooming together is an exercise in giving to and receiving from each other. Be willing to give, and be grateful for what you are given. Be willing to receive, and look for ways to give away a portion of what you have received. And look for a roommate who is willing to do likewise.

40 ❑ The Three *T*'s

In considering whether a person might make a good roommate, give some thought to the three *T*'s: taste, temperament, and togetherness.

Taste This refers to aesthetic matters, not biology. Ask about a potential roommate, Does this person appreciate the things in life that I appreciate? Does this person decorate his current space in a way that I find appealing? Taste refers to preferences of

- design (in furniture and fixtures especially). If you're into decorating with antiques and your potential roommate is into chrome, glass, and black leather, you may have a major conflict!

- color. Do you like brights, and she likes earth tones? Are you into lots of variety while she prefers monochromatic themes?

- texture and fabrics. Do you like softness and your potential roommate slickness? Do you prefer natural fibers and your potential roommate synthetics?

- amount of light. Are you a bright-and-light aficionado, and the other person prefers dimness and closed shades?

- music and need for sound. Are you a person who needs a certain kind of music to complete your environment? Does the other person like silence or prefer a dramatically different genre of music?

- foods. Are you a gourmet and your potential roommate a junk food junkie? No problem—unless you are planning to share meals and entertain together!

Temperament Much of compatibility relates to basic temperament. Are you a sunshine personality—a person who awakens happy and tends to remain optimistic regardless of the situation at hand? You are likely to be drained by a roommate who is moody, easily irritated, and continually pessimistic. The other person, conversely, is likely to be frustrated by your continual "up" attitude.

Are you a person who expends high energy? Are you always in gear and on the go? You may tend to find a low-energy roommate irksome, regarding him as lazy, unproductive, or boring. He'll likely regard you as being overcharged and on your way to a heart attack.

Are you a person of high drama—taking life's many facets seriously, with an eye toward continual engagement in the cosmic struggle? You'll likely find an easygoing, laid-back roommate to be uninteresting. She, on the other hand, may find that you tie her up in emotional knots she's never learned to make or undo!

Are you a leader? Are you comfortable having a roommate who doesn't care, doesn't notice, and doesn't seem interested in applauding your performances?

Are you cool, calm, collected, and consistently rational? You'll probably react negatively to a roommate who has temper flares, is easily ruffled, and responds emotionally to virtually everything.

In living with a person, you live with moods and personality, not simply physical presence.

Togetherness   You should consider the degree of togetherness that a roommate desires. Does your roommate like a few close friends around him at all times? Does he have a deep need for sharing intimately and extensively? Do you prefer more emotional distance and enjoy a wide circle of varied friends and acquaintances? If so, you may not find much common ground. You are likely to be irritated that your roommate always has other people in your shared space, or you may find your roommate's behavior to be too familiar. Your roommate, on the other hand, is likely to find you aloof, snobbish, and out of touch with people.

Openly discuss how much time and attention your roommate truly expects you to provide for the creation and sustenance of your relationship as roommates. Are you willing to give that time and attention? If not, recognize that you have different needs, and seek to find a more suitable roommate.

41 ❑ Remain Independent

Relationships can easily slide into a pattern in which one person becomes dominant, the other subordinant. If that happens, it's only a short step to the point where one person begins to expect the other person to lead or to follow. The result is usually that the subordinate, always-yielding person begins to experience lower self-esteem and a loss of self-respect. The always-in-charge person may easily become abusive and manipulative.

How can you avoid this unpleasant and emotionally unhealthy state in your relationship?

Choose Independence Continue to express your own opinions, make your own choices, set your own goals, make your own plans—and initiate them, voice them, and act on them. Take responsibility for yourself.

Even though you can and should be concerned about your roommate's general welfare, recognize that you are not responsible for controlling, manipulating, or coercing your roommate into doing anything that is against your roommate's will or desire.

Put On the Brakes   If you sense that you are being pushed (coerced or manipulated) into becoming a person's roommate, refuse to enter such a relationship. A roommate relationship needs to be entered into freely by both persons. It needs to be sustained without pressure to remain roommates.

Confront Unhealthy Trends   If your roommate threatens you, continually attempts to make you feel guilty or at fault in the relationship, routinely manipulates you into yielding to her will, or as a habit relies on you to make decisions regarding her behavior, confront the trend you sense. Without accusations, talk with your roommate about strategies you both might use to remain independent in your thinking, self-reliant in your behavior, and emotionally free.

42 ❏ Dating

Roommates everywhere seem to have one favorite topic of conversation: their love interests and dating relationships! As you share information with each other, remember these principles.

Keep Confidences Don't spread gossip about your roommate or retell what has been told to you. Don't pry for details or ask questions that might jeopardize your opinion about a third person.

Express Your Opinions Without Judgment If you feel that your roommate is engaging in behavior that may be injurious—either physically or emotionally—offer your opinion, but register your concern as just that, your opinion.

Set Your Own Boundaries As a roommate, you have a say in what activities take place in the space you share. Agree with your roommate in advance of your rooming together about what types of behavior will be off-limits in shared spaces. Your roommate should agree to abstain from behavior that you find offensive in your presence, to refrain from openly displaying posters, calendars, sculpture, artwork, or magazines that you find objection-able, and to refrain from certain topics that you don't wish to discuss.

If a roommate cannot agree to restrict or abstain from certain behaviors in your room or apartment, find another roommate.

Be Loyal to Your Roommate Don't steal your roommate's date. Sometimes in hearing all the wonderful attributes of a third person, a room-mate will begin to fantasize about having a relation-ship with that person. Find your own date. And don't attempt a relationship with your roommate's romantic interest until you are certain that your roommate is no longer interested in the person.

If you part company with a roommate for rea-sons related to dating or sexual behavior, do so with sealed lips. Don't tarnish your roommate's reputation. Allow your roommate the opportunity to change, and perhaps mature, without commen-tary.

43 ❑ Fighting Fair

Roommates will disagree. That's a fact of life that both need to realize. The critical issue is this: Can you fight fair and emerge as friendly coinhabitants of your shared space?

Disagreements and the Relationship In evaluating whether a person will make a good roommate, consider your past history with the person.

Do you ever disagree? If not, you probably aren't being honest with each other, you don't have much longevity as friends or don't communicate very deeply, or the relationship may be marred by manipulation. Reevaluate your relationship.

When you have a disagreement, is your discussion calm and rational, or is it marked by high emotion (for example, tears or thrown objects)? Do both stay focused on the issue, or do both interject stray issues or past accusations? Are voices raised? Is the atmosphere charged by hatred, intense anger, or bitterness?

How are your disagreements resolved? Does one person always win? Is a compromise reached, or does one person's desire always hold sway?

After a disagreement, what happens? Is the aftermath of a fight marked by pouting, silence, grudges, retaliation, revenge, or aftershocks of snide remarks? Or are both able to move forward?

Fair Fighting   Fair fighting is marked by these characteristics:

- Both parties refrain from physical blows.

- Both parties recognize that they are in disagreement, and they want to resolve that disagreement for mutual benefit.

- Both parties enter the fight recognizing that each is going to have to compromise to a greater or lesser extent.

- Both parties agree to approach the problem calmly, objectively, and rationally. They choose to keep the discussion focused only on the problem and not on each other's personality or character flaws, on previous disagreements, or on side issues.

- Both parties avoid using the words *always* and *never*.

- Both parties are solution oriented. They want to see a new pattern of behavior established, about which both can agree. Out of disagreement, both parties seek agreement.

- Both parties agree that after the fight, they will move forward in harmony, hold no grudges, and refuse to seek revenge.

- Both parties recognize that they can agree to disagree—that two people will invariably hold differing views and that this is healthy, not unhealthy, human behavior.

- Both parties recognize that disagreements over procedure, behavior, or choices that affect the rooming-together relationship do not invalidate a person's value or right to be treated with dignity.

- Both parties refrain from dragging other people into the disagreement or insisting that friends take sides.

Agree with a potential roommate that you will confront problems that arise between you and that you will seek to fight fair. Recognize that disagreements can lead to greater personal growth and stronger relationships if the fighting is fair and both parties want the relationship to continue.

44 ❏ Get References

References and recommendations are standard fare when one is seeking employment, placement in a private school or an institution with limited enrollment or access, or appointment to a position that is subject to public scrutiny.

You will have a financial arrangement with a roommate. You will give this person a portion of your limited space and time. You will be evaluated by your superiors, family, and peers—in part—on your choice of a roommate and your relationship with one. You will be learning valuable life lessons from and with this person. It is not at all unreasonable to expect, therefore, that you would—and should—seek the advice of others before settling on a roommate.

Previous Roommates Have a conversation with the person's current or previous roommate. You don't need to gossip or seek to unearth all of the possible negatives about the person. Just ask some basic questions: "What is it like to live with this person? Have you ever felt uncomfortable? Would you live with this person again if given the opportunity?" And then listen closely.

Talk to the person's siblings, if possible. Patterns of behavior in a person's life are usually long-standing. Ask, "What was it like growing up with this person?" The sibling is likely to tell you more than you wanted to know!

Talk to some people who know the person well. Why aren't they rooming with the person? Their reasons may not affect your decision; still, you may find their reasons insightful and beneficial.

Visits Spend some time with the person in his current living space. Are you comfortable there? Can you relax in the person's presence and in the environment she has created? Does anything make you nervous or uneasy? Isolate your concerns and fears.

Prior Living Conditions It's important to know if a potential roommate has lived in an environment that is decidedly different from the one you will be sharing.

- Is the person from another country? Is he accustomed to American-style furniture, facilities, foods, and customs?

- Has the person been a hermit?

- Has the person grown up as an only child, lived in a boarding school, had a luxurious lifestyle complete with maids and chauffeurs, or been part of a very strict religious sect?

These situations are not necessarily detrimental, but they can and do affect the way in which a person relates to a roommate and to a shared living space. Better to find out and deal with issues that you suspect may arise than to enter the relationship naively.

45 ❏ Don't Speak for Your Roommate

Don't Presume Don't presume to know what your roommate is thinking.

Don't presume to know what decision your roommate will make.

Don't attempt to forecast your roommate's future behavior.

Don't Second-Guess Don't second-guess your roommate's feelings (especially in conversations with his girlfriend or her boyfriend).

Don't psychoanalyze your roommate's motives or past behavior.

Don't Say It Don't accept invitations on behalf of your roommate, obligate him, or make promises that he will act in a certain way (or even that he will return phone calls).

Even if you know your roommate's opinion on a particular topic or about a specific person, don't voice it.

Don't Assume Responsibility Expect your roommate to be responsible for her decisions, choices, beliefs, values, and the behavior that results from them. Refuse to convey messages on behalf of your roommate or to act as an intermediary in negotiating dates, providing excuses, or justifying bad behavior.

Let your roommate speak for himself.

46 ❑ Put It Where It Belongs

In most rooming-together situations, space is limited. Thus, everything probably has a place, and nothing is without a designated place. Don't force your roommate to spend what can seem to be endless frustrating time searching for the item that has been used and then "hidden" in a foreign location.

Return Policy If you take a mutually shared item from your room or apartment, leave a note saying so—citing where you have taken it and when you expect to return it.

If you lend an item (of your own, never your roommate's unless you have permission) that is normally a part of the shared utensils, furniture, or supply of sundries, let your roommate know what you have done and when you expect the return of the item.

No Hide-and-Seek Decide in advance with your roommate where certain tools and supplies will be kept. Include among the items such things as toilet bowl plunger, flyswatter, scissors and tape, needle and thread, and any other item that you can identify as falling into the "you need it right away and don't have time to hunt for it" category.

Decide on a place where you will keep keys to shared spaces, cabinets, or closets. Choose a place where both will put the day's mail, newspaper, and phone messages. Have a place where you habitually keep your shopping list (for supplies and food items that are shared), receipts, and your agreement book. You may want to invest in a small bulletin board as a means of coordinating your communication.

In Case of Emergency Keep emergency numbers posted where they can be found quickly and easily. The same goes for emergency medical procedures (perhaps best taped to the inside of a bathroom cabinet).

47 ❑ Be Security-Minded

You may trust the world and feel no need to lock your door or secure your windows. As a roommate, however, your concern must never be solely for your own things or safety.

Agree with your roommate that each will do the best to preserve the other's life and material goods.

Locks Lock your room or apartment when you leave it. Make sure that all windows and patio doors are closed and secure. You may want to invest together in dead bolt locks or secure window fasteners and screens. Depending on your neighborhood and the amount of your material goods, you may also want to invest in alarm systems for your home and automobiles.

Keys Keep track of your keys. Don't give duplicate keys to friends. Don't loan out keys. Don't hide them outside your room or apartment.

Privacy Be very cautious in giving out information related to your address, your schedule, or your roommate's schedule. An effective security measure is random behavior, avoiding predictable routines. Make sure that you have adequate window coverings.

General Security   If you are going to be away for the weekend, use timers on lamps. Have someone pick up your mail and newspaper (or stop delivery for the days you will be away).

Make sure the entrance to your apartment or room is well lit. Park your car in as secure a location as possible. Is the path from your car to your dwelling adequately lit and as safe as possible?

Check that smoke alarms are in good working order.

Valuables   Expensive jewelry, cashier's checks, negotiable bonds, passports, or any other item that you consider to be irreplaceable or extremely valuable—and that you definitely wouldn't want to lose in a fire, theft, or natural catastrophe—should be stored in a safe-deposit box.

If you own valuable items of furniture, silver flatware or serving pieces, or artwork that you can live without during your years in a dorm or apartment, leave the items at home with your parents.

Don't leave valuables—including cash—in plain sight.

Insurance   Consider investing in renter's insurance as a part of your mutually shared expenses.

48 ❑ Move In

Don't straddle the fence. If you decide to move in with another person, move in quickly, efficiently, and completely.

Don't leave a potential roommate hanging, wondering if you are moving in or moving out. Set a date for moving in, and give a date when you expect to be completely moved out.

Make your moves expediently. Don't stretch out the moving process over weeks or months. Get in and get settled. Get organized and get out. Make your move as smooth as possible, with the least amount of disruption for your roommate.

Don't expect your roommate to help you with your move—either in or out. That's your responsibility. Don't take over shared space while you sort out things or decide how you want to arrange your personal space.

Make arrangements for your mail to be forwarded by the post office. Send out change of address forms (including your new phone number) well in advance of your move.

Arrive Emotionally Don't talk incessantly about the place you used to live or the roommate you used to have (especially in comparative terms that may leave your present roommate feeling inferior).

Introduce yourself to your neighbors. Find your way around the neighborhood. Establish a new routine. Expect your new home to be different from your previous one, and work diligently to adapt to your new routine and new surroundings.

Unpack your luggage. Unload the boxes. Occupy your new home both emotionally and literally. Your roommate will feel a lot less tenuous about your presence. And you probably will feel more settled in spirit, too.

Don't threaten to move out unless you are serious and willing to follow through. Don't talk about your desire for a better place or a new roommate until you are truly willing to make a move.

A Space Prepared Prior to moving in with a roommate who is already occupying a space, make certain that sufficient room has been cleared for you—especially closet, drawer, and storage space. Don't move in until you have a place to move in to!

49 ❑ Stay Active

It's easy for roommates to isolate themselves from the outside world. This frequently happens when two close friends decide to room together or when two people move away from a dorm setting into their own apartment.

Stay involved with the outside world.

Go out with friends other than your roommate.

Invite people into your shared space (within the general provisions of your agreement together and as long as your roommate is comfortable with the guest list).

Develop interests and sources of information other than your roommate.

You'll be far more likely to develop a healthy emotional relationship with your roommate When both people are active, involved, and committed to activities and relationships beyond their own, they have a much greater likelihood of developing an interdependent, accommodating roommate relationship.

You'll feel much less "root bound" in your room or apartment It's both psychologically and physically healthy for a person to be actively engaged in life outside the confines of a room or apartment.

You'll be much better prepared emotionally when the time comes for the two of you to go your separate ways

Life will be much more interesting for both of you When each person brings new information, insights, and people to a relationship, both people have a greater opportunity to learn, grow, and expand their horizons.

Don't limit yourself to your roommate relationship or to your shared room or apartment. Embrace a larger world.

50 ❏ Be True to Yourself

You can't help being influenced by a roommate, and vice versa. Roommate pressure is perhaps the most intense form of peer pressure. One of your foremost challenges in a roommate relationship will be to find a balance between being open to new ideas and opinions and remaining true to your moral code and your sense of personal identity. In the main, choose to be true to yourself.

Hold Fast to What You Believe to Be True Even as you question, doubt, and struggle to refine what you believe as a person, hold fast to those things that you have come to know deep in your heart as true. Don't let anyone talk you out of your faith, the love you feel for your family, the respect you have for authority, or the goals you have set for your life.

Say No Say no to things that are unhealthful, abusive, demeaning, stereotyping, limiting, defaming, impoverishing, segregating, or illegal. Keep in mind that you don't need to experience certain things to have opinions about them or to recognize them as evil.

Say Yes Say yes to things that give you deep inner joy, are fulfilling, cause you to giggle without constraint, and about which you can communicate openly. Never be ashamed of innocence.

The more you are true to yourself, the more you give your roommate the freedom to be true to himself. Support each other in your shared quests for the best that life holds. Foster a shared desire to find your niches in life and achieve your full potential within them. It's not unusual to find that mutually supportive roommates walk very different paths but enjoy equal success along the way.

Allow genuine compassion to take root in your heart for your roommate. Be quick to forgive. Find ways to express kindness and generosity. In so doing, you will develop your character as a person even as you help your roommate.

51 ❑ Go Beyond Your Agreement— Positively!

Much of your agreement with your roommate will cover specific behaviors—paying bills, scrubbing and scouring, dividing the workload, making decisions about what will and won't be considered acceptable behavior in your apartment.

Beyond the rules of a relationship lies an entire realm perhaps best described as the heart of a relationship.

Love Choose to love your roommate with the good-hearted love that exists between friends. This type of love is an act of the will, not a syrupy emotion or a sexual overture. It is rooted in giving and sharing.

Give Choose to give to your roommate. Look intentionally for opportunities to help your roommate, encourage your roommate, build up your roommate's self-esteem, or do something nice for your roommate. Insist that she get away from the books and go for a twenty-minute walk with you as a study break. Fix your roommate a midnight snack to help him through his preparation for a big exam. Invite her to go along on an outing with your friends. Volunteer to run an errand when you see that he is pressed for time.

Be There   Stand by your roommate in times of sorrow. Lend a shoulder to lean on. Listen with your heart. Go with your roommate to the funeral home, the cemetery, the hospital room. Don't ignore a roommate's broken heart; rather, find ways to help mend it.

Share   Choose to share the joys of life with your roommate. Surprise her with a bunch of flowers for her room. Share funny anecdotes and jokes that you hear. Find a game that both of you enjoy—whether shooting hoops or playing chess—and take play breaks together.

Help   Assist your roommate in whatever ways you can to live a healthy, balanced, well-rounded life. You'll find your own life to be better balanced and your relationship healthier.

52 ❑ Peaceful Good-byes and Friendly Futures

Throw a Party When the time comes to part company, choose to turn what may be a sad time into a celebration. It may be an end-of-the-year or end-of-the-term party in which both of you are celebrating. It may be a party to celebrate the next new exciting chapter in your roommate's life—perhaps marriage, graduation, a new job in another city, further study in graduate school.

In your final days together as roommates, spend a few moments reflecting about the good times you've shared and how both have changed as people. Thank your roommate for the lessons you've learned from him.

Anticipate a good future for both of you. Don't wallow in your parting. Instead, choose to view the closure of your time together as a milestone in your growth as individuals.

Part in Peace If your parting is the result of a disagreement or irreconcilable differences, do your very best to establish peace between you. Apologize to your roommate for your part in the failure of the relationship (even if you see the disaster as being totally the other person's fault). Don't devalue the person. Express your hope that the person will have a more satisfying roommate relationship in the future. Wish her well, and be genuine in your expressions of goodwill.

Once you and a roommate have parted ways, avoid the tendency to tell your former roommate's secrets or to gossip about him in any way. Keep your relationship private both during and after your time of living together.

Don't overanalyze or become overly sentimental about your relationship. Be grateful for the time you had together—to learn more about life and about human nature in general, to learn more about yourself in particular, and to grow in your ability to lead a mature adult life.

And finally, recognize that even though you are no longer roommates sharing a room, house, or apartment, you will continue to be two people sharing the same planet. As such, you are still in relationship—however distant—and will be all your lives.

Be gentle with each other as you live together, as you part, and after you part. Life will be more peaceful and joyful for both of you.

❑ Conclusion

Buy your new roommate a copy of this book, if at all possible, prior to your rooming together. It will give you a common point of reference as you discuss various facets of your living together. It will also provide an authority to which you might appeal in citing problems or attempting to express difficulties in a relationship.